INVENTIONS AND DISCOVERY

MADAM C. J. WALKER AND
NEW COSMETICS

by Katherine Krohn

illustrated by Richard Dominguez, Dave Hoover,

Bill Anderson, and Charles Barnett III

Consultant:

A'Lelia Bundles

Great-great-granddaughter of Madam C. J. Walker

Author, *On Her Own Ground: The Life and Times of
Madam C. J. Walker*

Capstone

press

Mankato, Minnesota

Graphic Library is published by Capstone Press,
151 Good Counsel Drive, P.O. Box 669, Mankato, Minnesota 56002.
www.capstonepress.com

Printed in the United States of America

1 2 3 4 5 6 11 10 09 08 07 06

Library of Congress Cataloging-in-Publication Data

Krohn, Katherine E.

Madam C. J. Walker and new cosmetics / by Katherine Krohn; illustrated by Richard Dominguez . . . [et al.].

p. cm.—(Graphic library. Inventions and discovery)

Includes bibliographical references and index.

ISBN-13: 978-0-7368-6485-5 (hardcover)

ISBN-10: 0-7368-6485-7 (hardcover)

ISBN-13: 978-0-7368-9647-4 (softcover pbk.)

ISBN-10: 0-7368-9647-3 (softcover pbk.)

1. Walker, C. J., Madam, 1867–1919—Juvenile literature. 2. African American women executives—Biography—Juvenile literature. 3. Cosmetics industry—United States—History—Juvenile literature. 4. Women millionaires—United States—Biography—Juvenile literature. I. Dominguez, Richard. II. Title. III. Series.

HD9970.5.C672K76 2007

338.7'66855092—dc22 2006004080

Summary: In graphic novel format, tells the story of Madam C. J. Walker, who invented a line of African American hair products and cosmetics that helped her become the first self-made female millionaire of any race.

Designer
Alison Thiele

Colorist
Benjamin Hunzeker

Editor
Christine Peterson

Editor's note: Direct quotations from primary sources are indicated by a yellow background.

Direct quotations appear on the following pages:
Page 21, from Madam C. J. Walker's speech before the 1912 convention of the National Negro Business League, as recorded by the NNBL; page 23, from a 1913 speech by Madam C. J. Walker; as published in *On Her Own Ground: The Life and Times of Madam C. J. Walker*, by A'Lelia Bundles (New York: Scribner, 2001).

TABLE OF CONTENTS

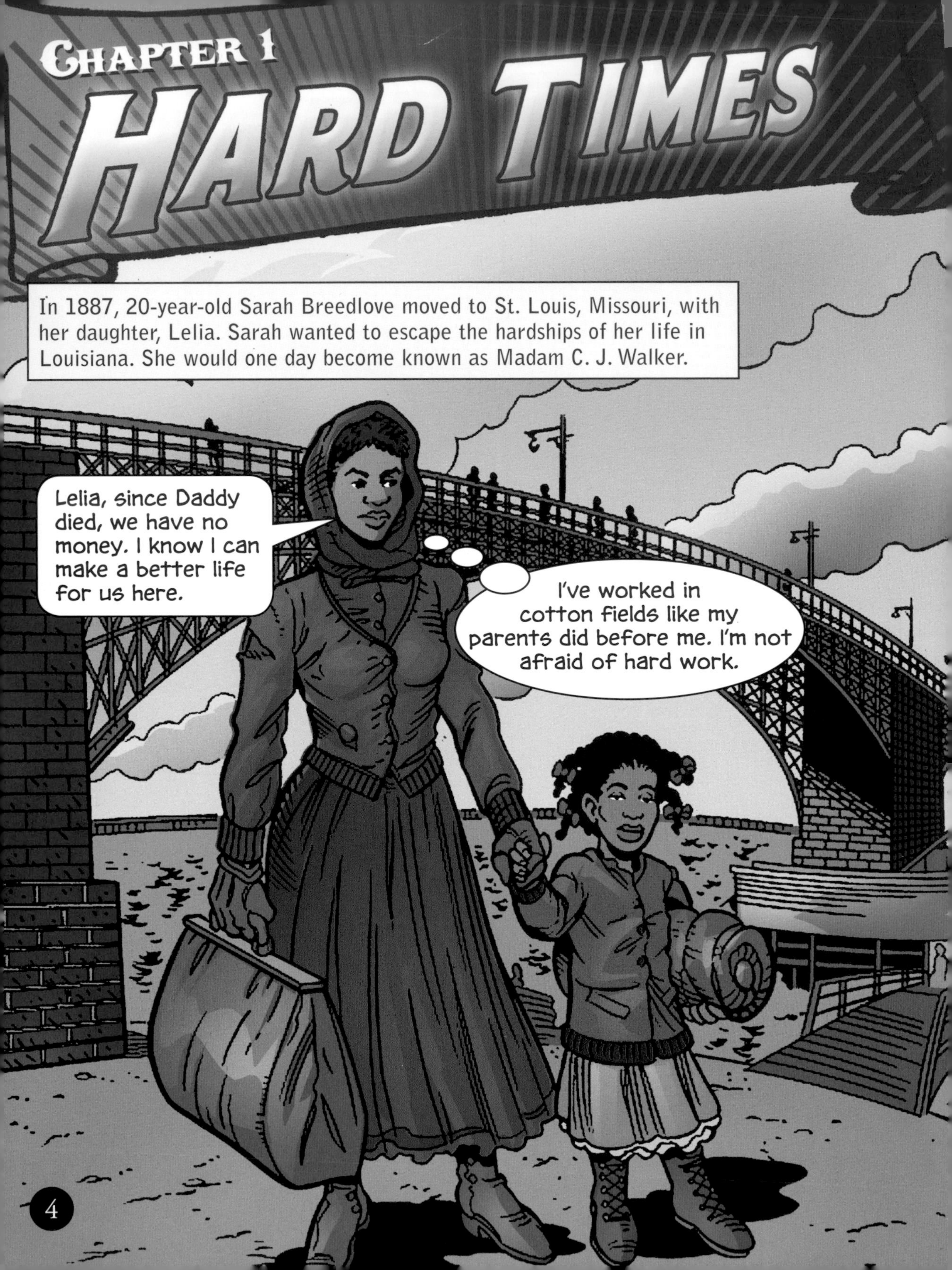
CHAPTER 1
HARD TIMES
In 1887, 20-year-old Sarah Breedlove moved to St. Louis, Missouri, with her daughter, Lelia. Sarah wanted to escape the hardships of her life in Louisiana. She would one day become known as Madam C. J. Walker.
Lelia, since Daddy died, we have no money. I know I can make a better life for us here.
I've worked in cotton fields like my parents did before me. I'm not afraid of hard work.

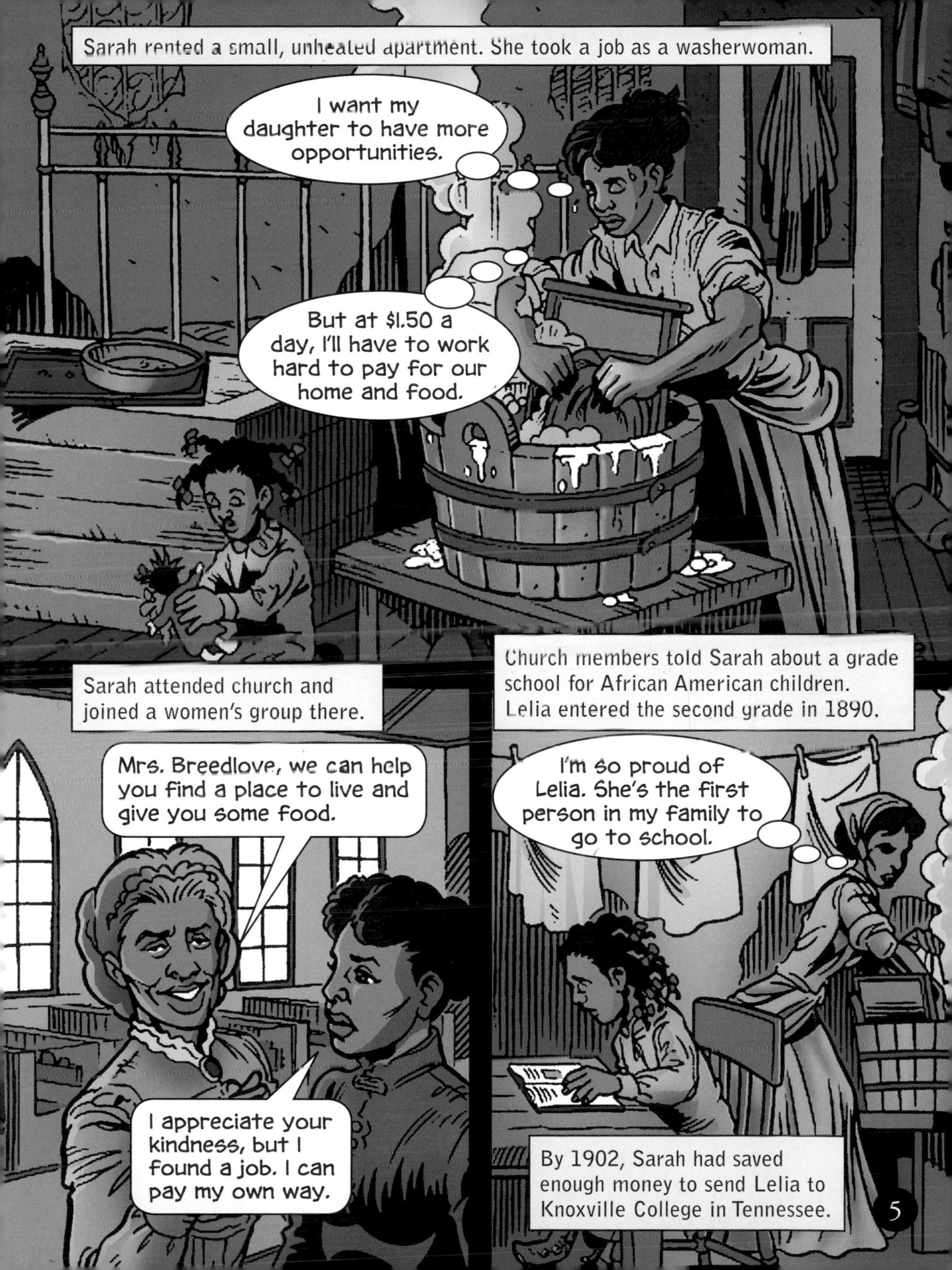
Sarah rented a small, unheated apartment. She took a job as a washerwoman.
I want my daughter to have more opportunities.
But at $1.50 a day, I'll have to work hard to pay for our home and food.
Sarah attended church and joined a women's group there.
Mrs. Breedlove, we can help you find a place to live and give you some food.
I appreciate your kindness, but I found a job. I can pay my own way.
Church members told Sarah about a grade school for African American children. Lelia entered the second grade in 1890.
I'm so proud of Lelia. She's the first person in my family to go to school.
By 1902, Sarah had saved enough money to send Lelia to Knoxville College in Tennessee.

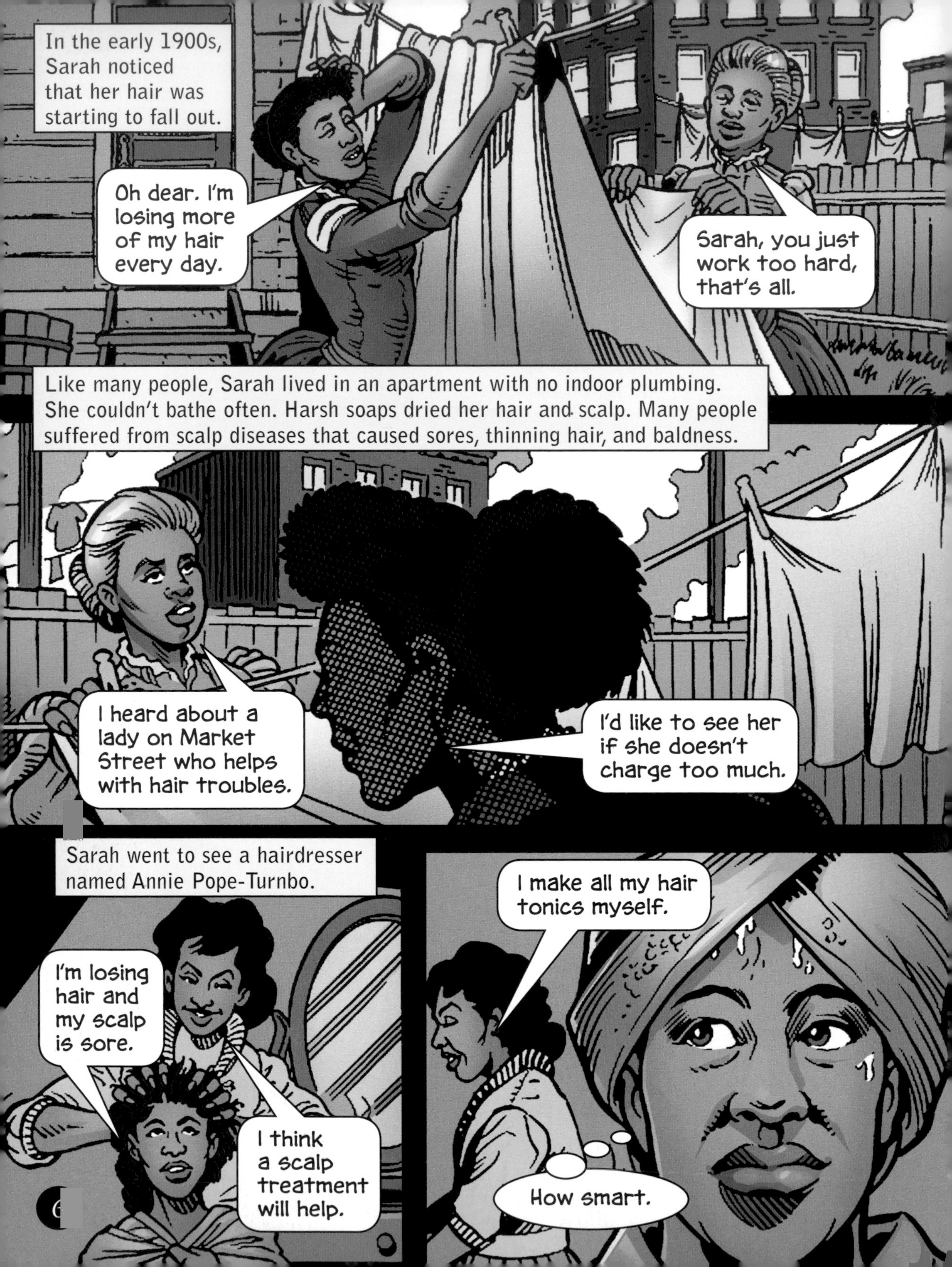
In the early 1900s, Sarah noticed that her hair was starting to fall out.
Oh dear. I'm losing more of my hair every day.
Sarah, you just work too hard, that's all.
Like many people, Sarah lived in an apartment with no indoor plumbing. She couldn't bathe often. Harsh soaps dried her hair and scalp. Many people suffered from scalp diseases that caused sores, thinning hair, and baldness.
I heard about a lady on Market Street who helps with hair troubles.
I'd like to see her if she doesn't charge too much.
Sarah went to see a hairdresser named Annie Pope-Turnbo.
I'm losing hair and my scalp is sore.
I think a scalp treatment will help.
I make all my hair tonics myself.
How smart.

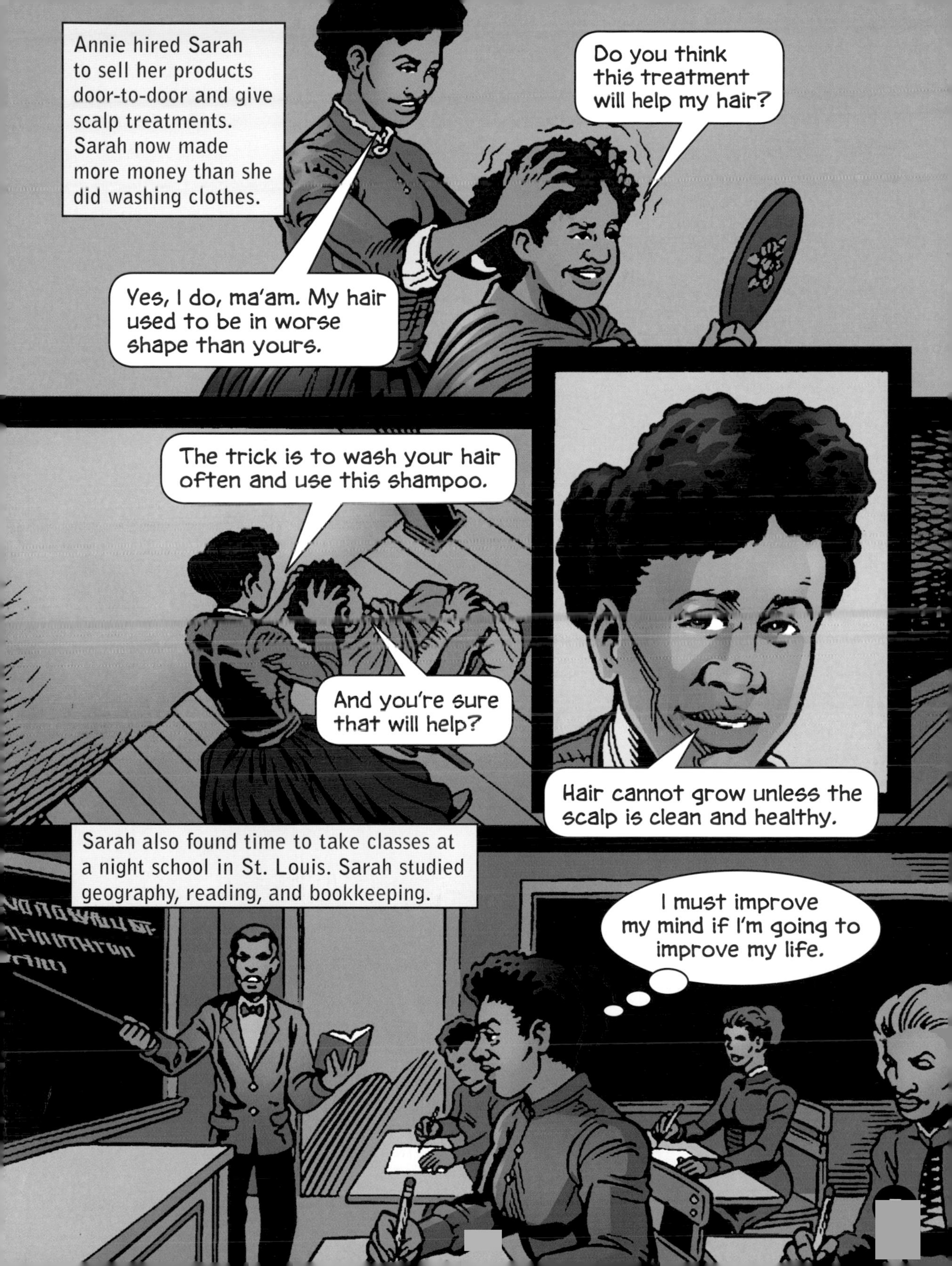
Annie hired Sarah to sell her products door-to-door and give scalp treatments. Sarah now made more money than she did washing clothes.
Do you think this treatment will help my hair?
Yes, I do, ma'am. My hair used to be in worse shape than yours.
The trick is to wash your hair often and use this shampoo.
And you're sure that will help?
Hair cannot grow unless the scalp is clean and healthy.
Sarah also found time to take classes at a night school in St. Louis. Sarah studied geography, reading, and bookkeeping.
I must improve my mind if I'm going to improve my life.

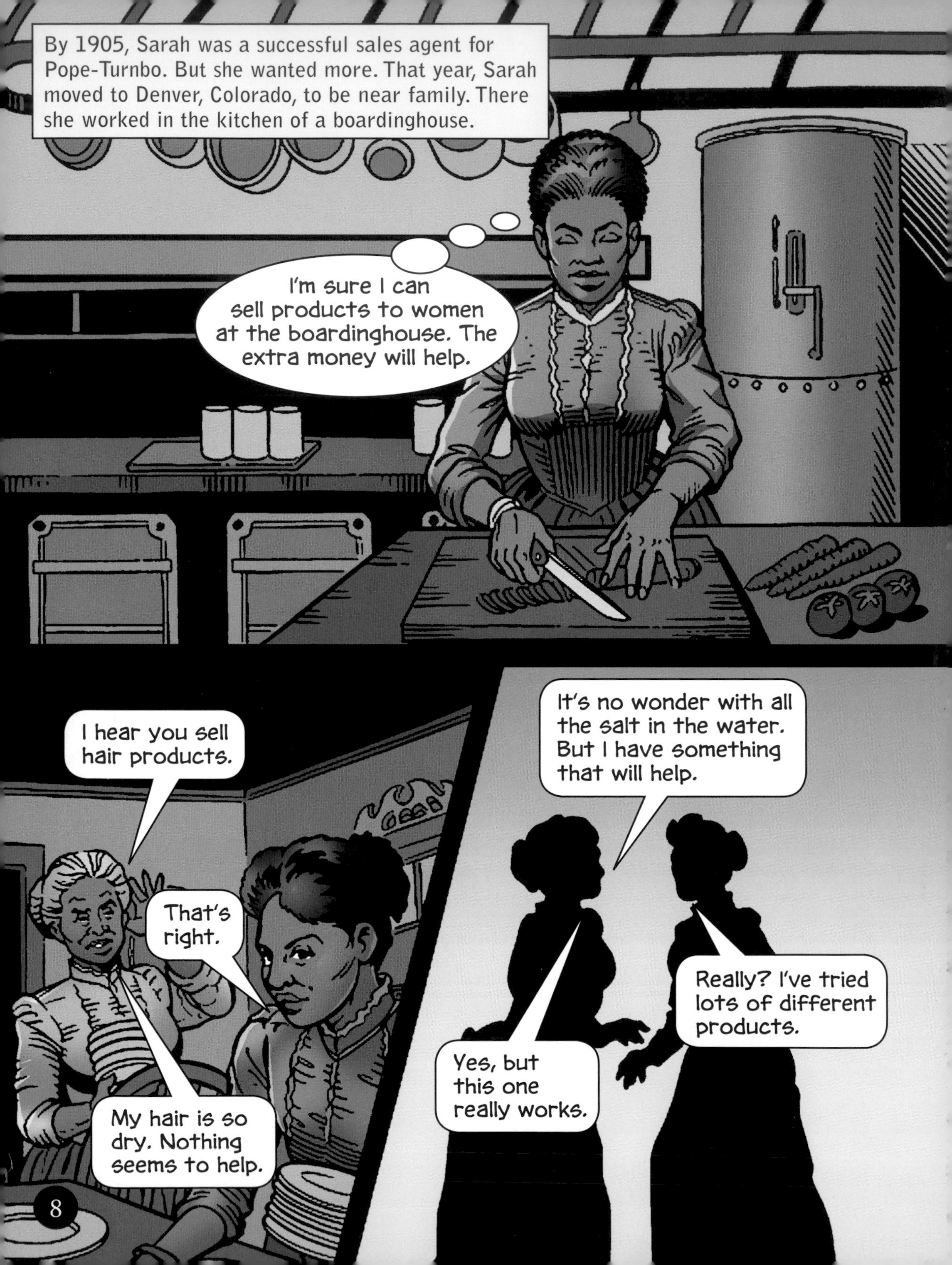
By 1905, Sarah was a successful sales agent for Pope-Turnbo. But she wanted more. That year, Sarah moved to Denver, Colorado, to be near family. There she worked in the kitchen of a boardinghouse.
I'm sure I can sell products to women at the boardinghouse. The extra money will help.
I hear you sell hair products.
That's right.
My hair is so dry. Nothing seems to help.
It's no wonder with all the salt in the water. But I have something that will help.
Really? I've tried lots of different products.
Yes, but this one really works.

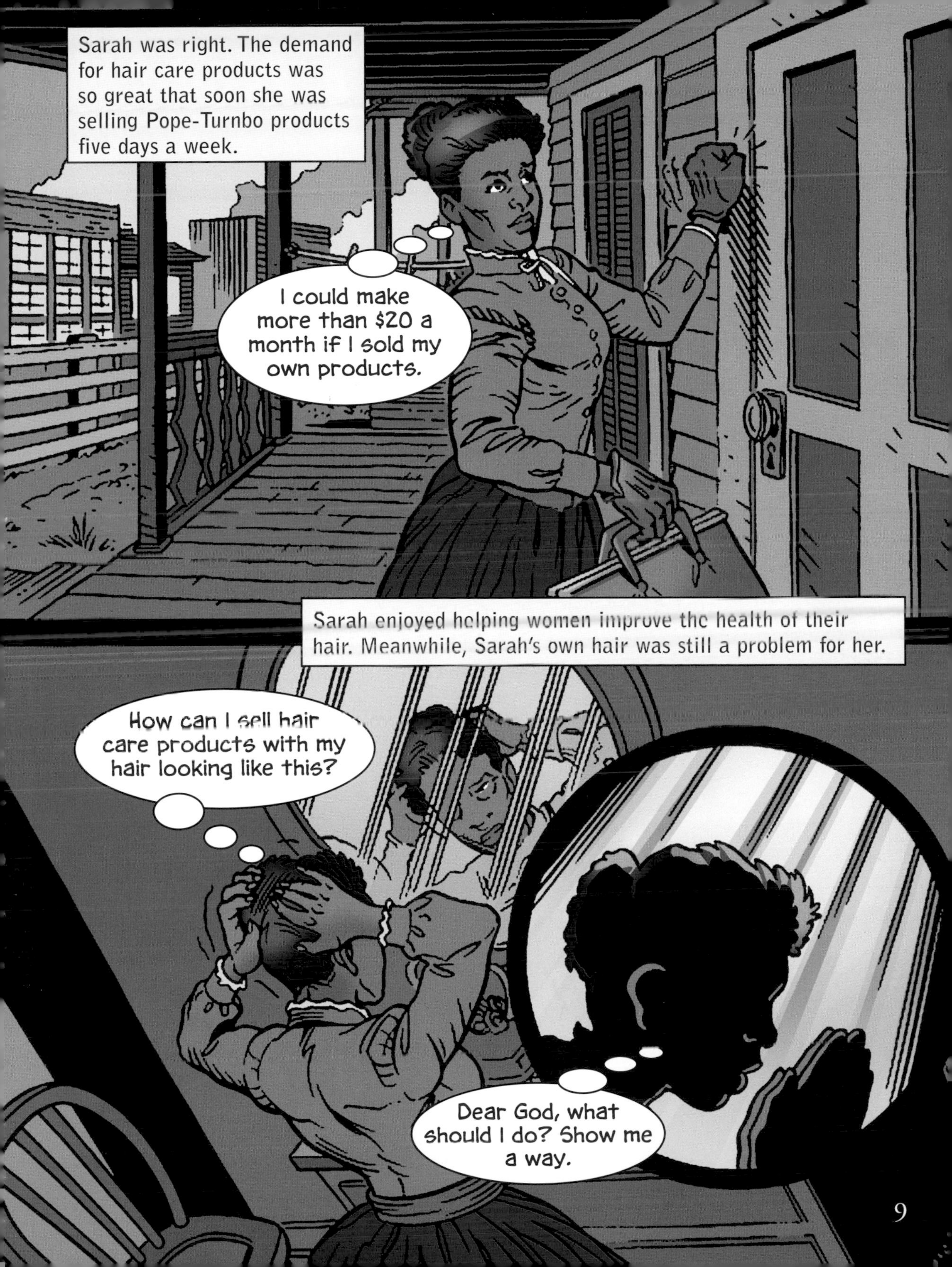

Sarah was right. The demand for hair care products was so great that soon she was selling Pope-Turnbo products five days a week.
I could make more than $20 a month if I sold my own products.
Sarah enjoyed helping women improve the health of their hair. Meanwhile, Sarah's own hair was still a problem for her.
How can I sell hair care products with my hair looking like this?
Dear God, what should I do? Show me a way.

Chapter 2

Following a Dream

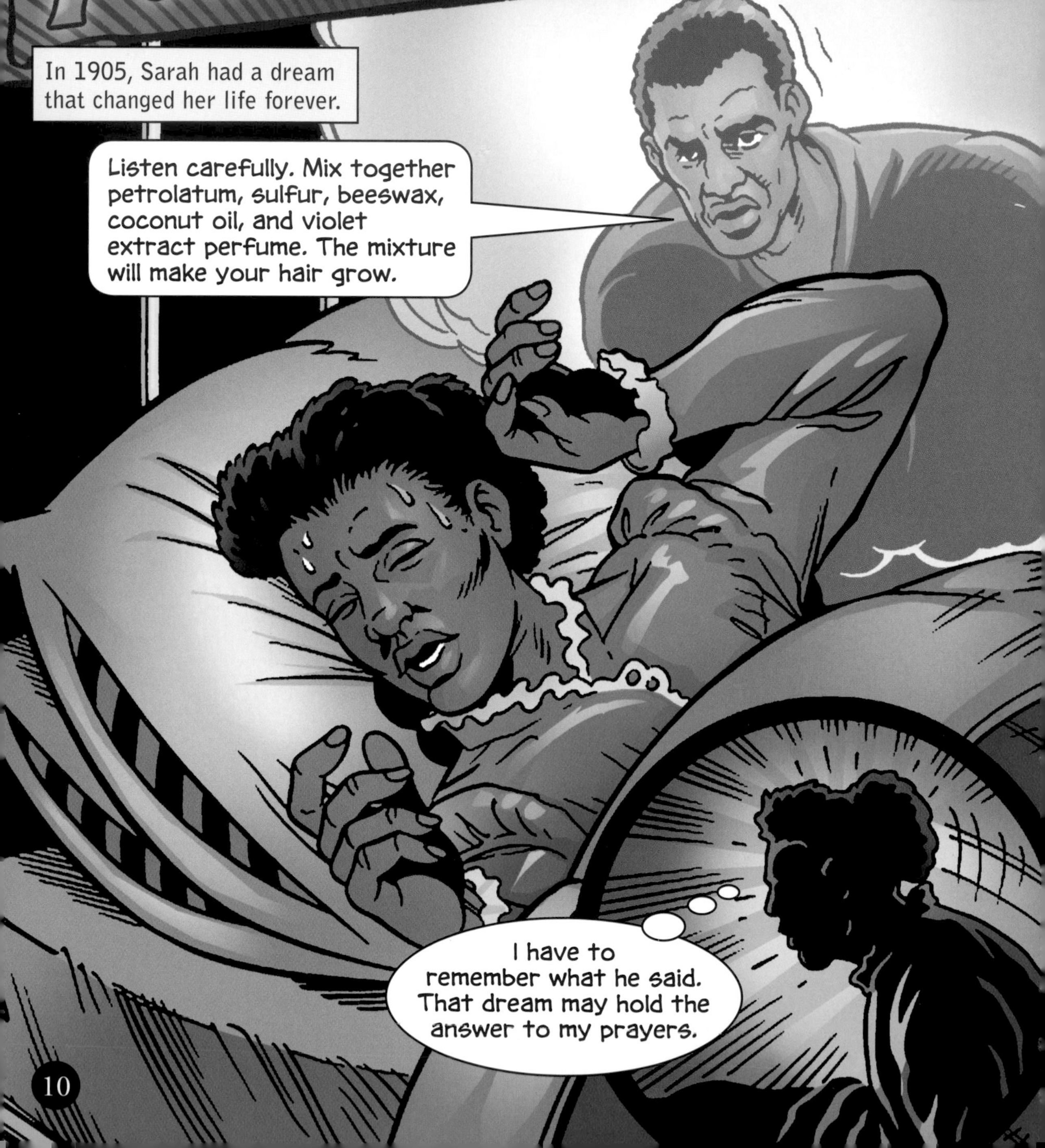
In 1905, Sarah had a dream that changed her life forever.
Listen carefully. Mix together petrolatum, sulfur, beeswax, coconut oil, and violet extract perfume. The mixture will make your hair grow.
I have to remember what he said. That dream may hold the answer to my prayers.

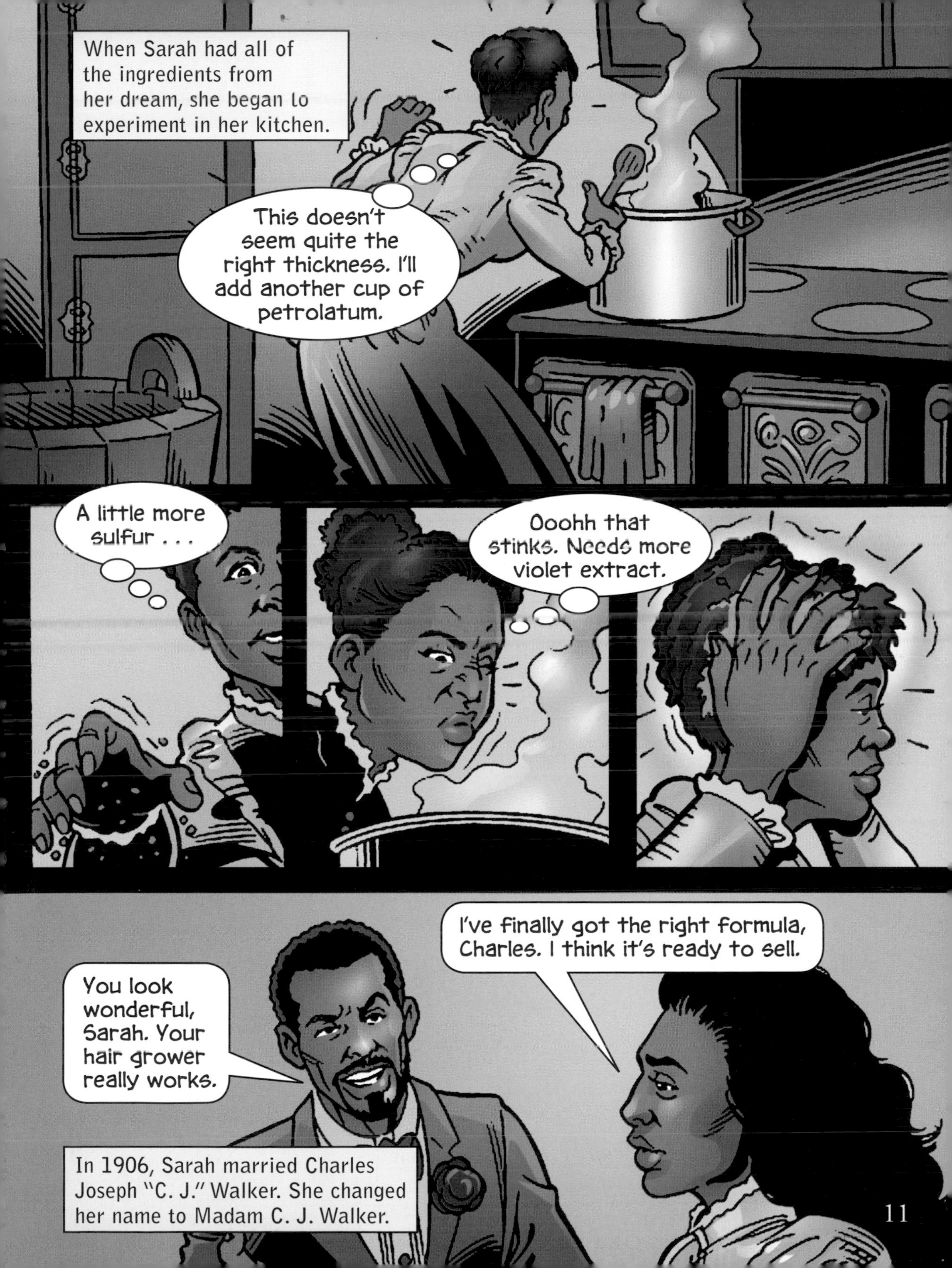
When Sarah had all of the ingredients from her dream, she began to experiment in her kitchen.
This doesn't seem quite the right thickness. I'll add another cup of petrolatum.
A little more sulfur . . .
Ooohh that stinks. Needs more violet extract.
I've finally got the right formula, Charles. I think it's ready to sell.
You look wonderful, Sarah. Your hair grower really works.
In 1906, Sarah married Charles Joseph "C. J." Walker. She changed her name to Madam C. J. Walker.

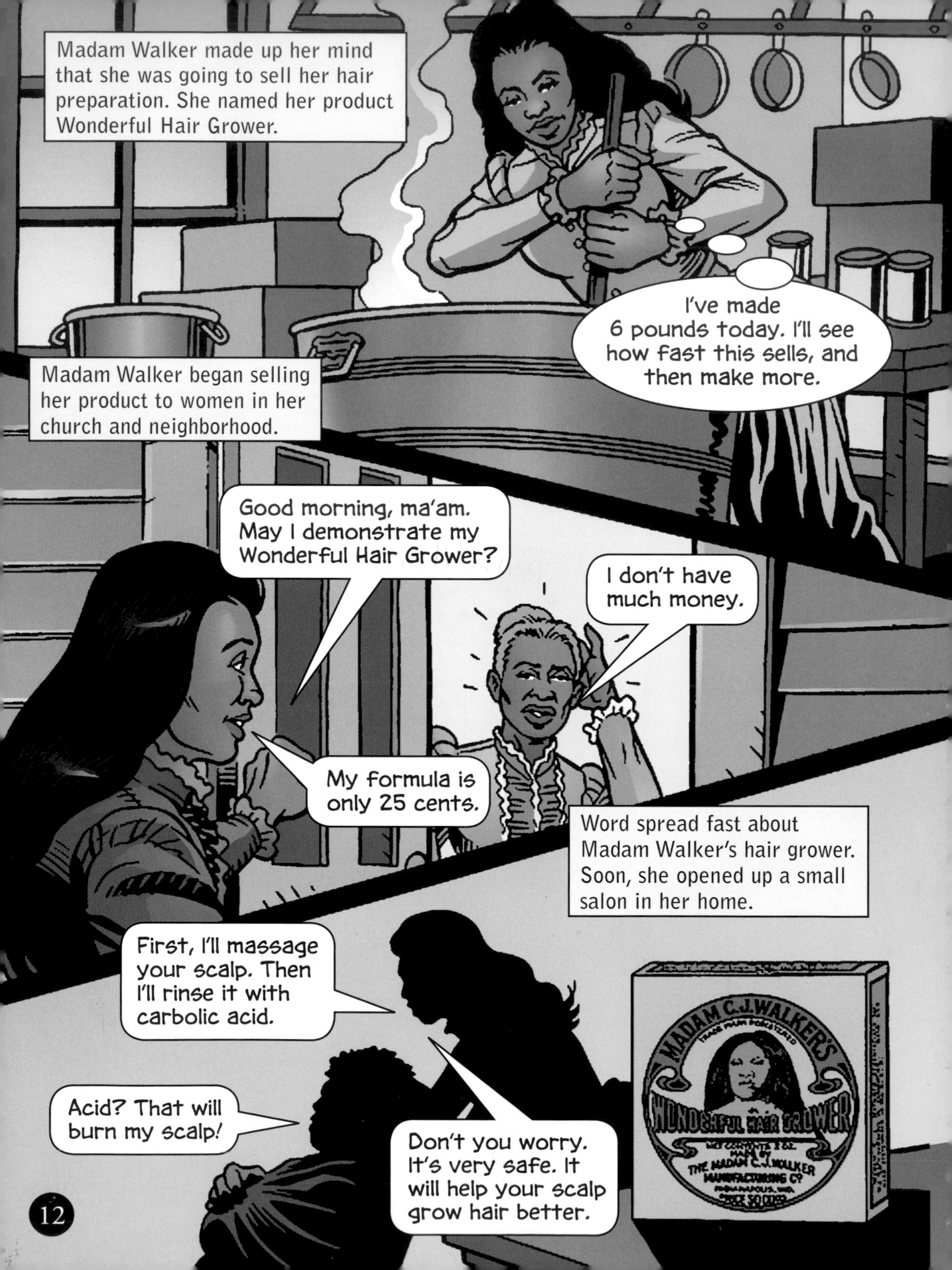

Madam Walker made up her mind that she was going to sell her hair preparation. She named her product Wonderful Hair Grower.
I've made 6 pounds today. I'll see how fast this sells, and then make more.
Madam Walker began selling her product to women in her church and neighborhood.
Good morning, ma'am. May I demonstrate my Wonderful Hair Grower?
I don't have much money.
My formula is only 25 cents.
Word spread fast about Madam Walker's hair grower. Soon, she opened up a small salon in her home.
First, I'll massage your scalp. Then I'll rinse it with carbolic acid.
Acid? That will burn my scalp!
Don't you worry. It's very safe. It will help your scalp grow hair better.
MADAM C.J. WALKER'S
WONDERFUL HAIR GROWER
THE MADAM C.J. WALKER MANUFACTURING CO.

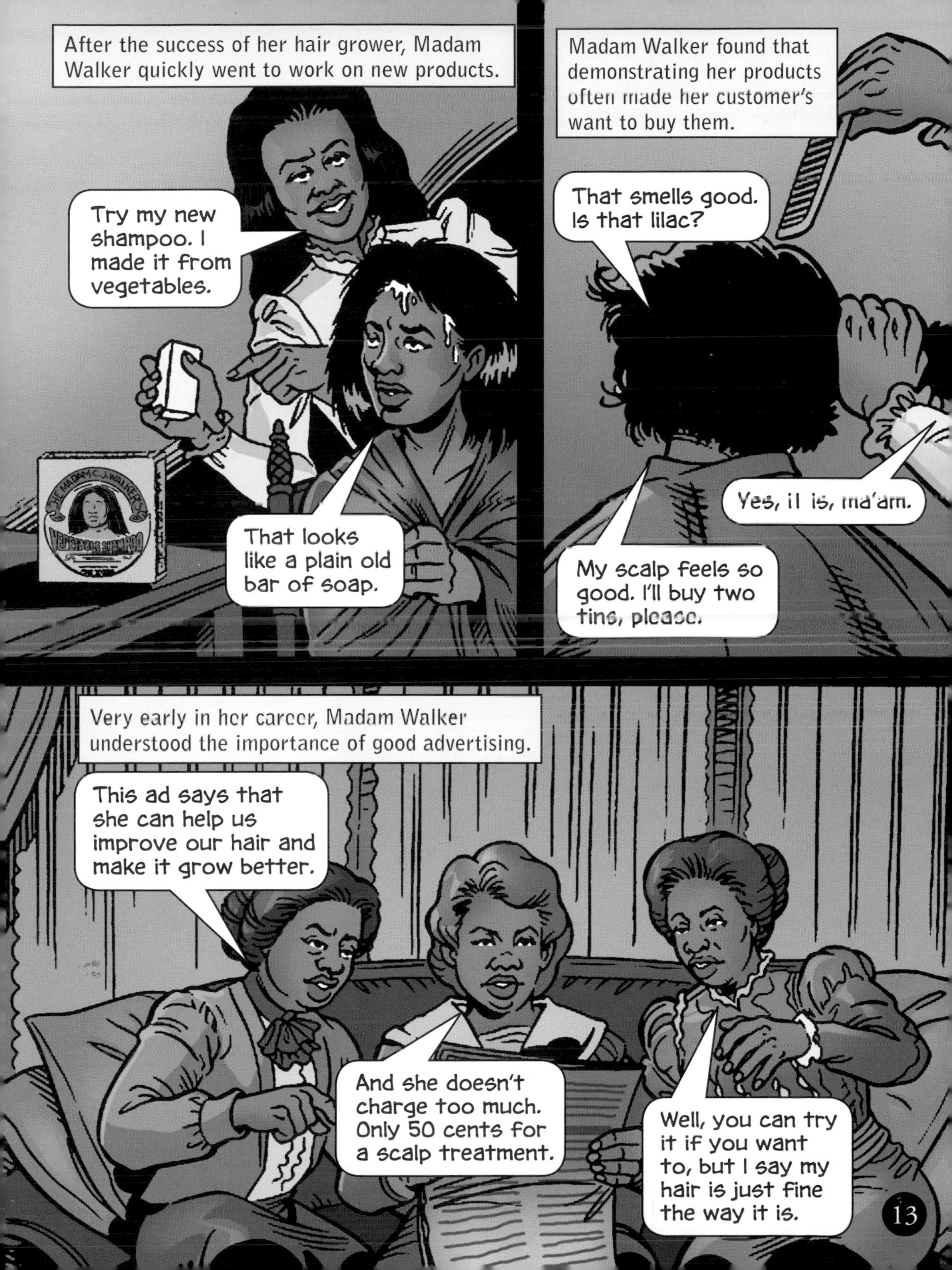
After the success of her hair grower, Madam Walker quickly went to work on new products.
Try my new shampoo. I made it from vegetables.
THE MADAM C. J. WALKER'S VEGETABLE SHAMPOO
That looks like a plain old bar of soap.
Madam Walker found that demonstrating her products often made her customer's want to buy them.
That smells good. Is that lilac?
Yes, it is, ma'am.
My scalp feels so good. I'll buy two tins, please.
Very early in her career, Madam Walker understood the importance of good advertising.
This ad says that she can help us improve our hair and make it grow better.
And she doesn't charge too much. Only 50 cents for a scalp treatment.
Well, you can try it if you want to, but I say my hair is just fine the way it is.

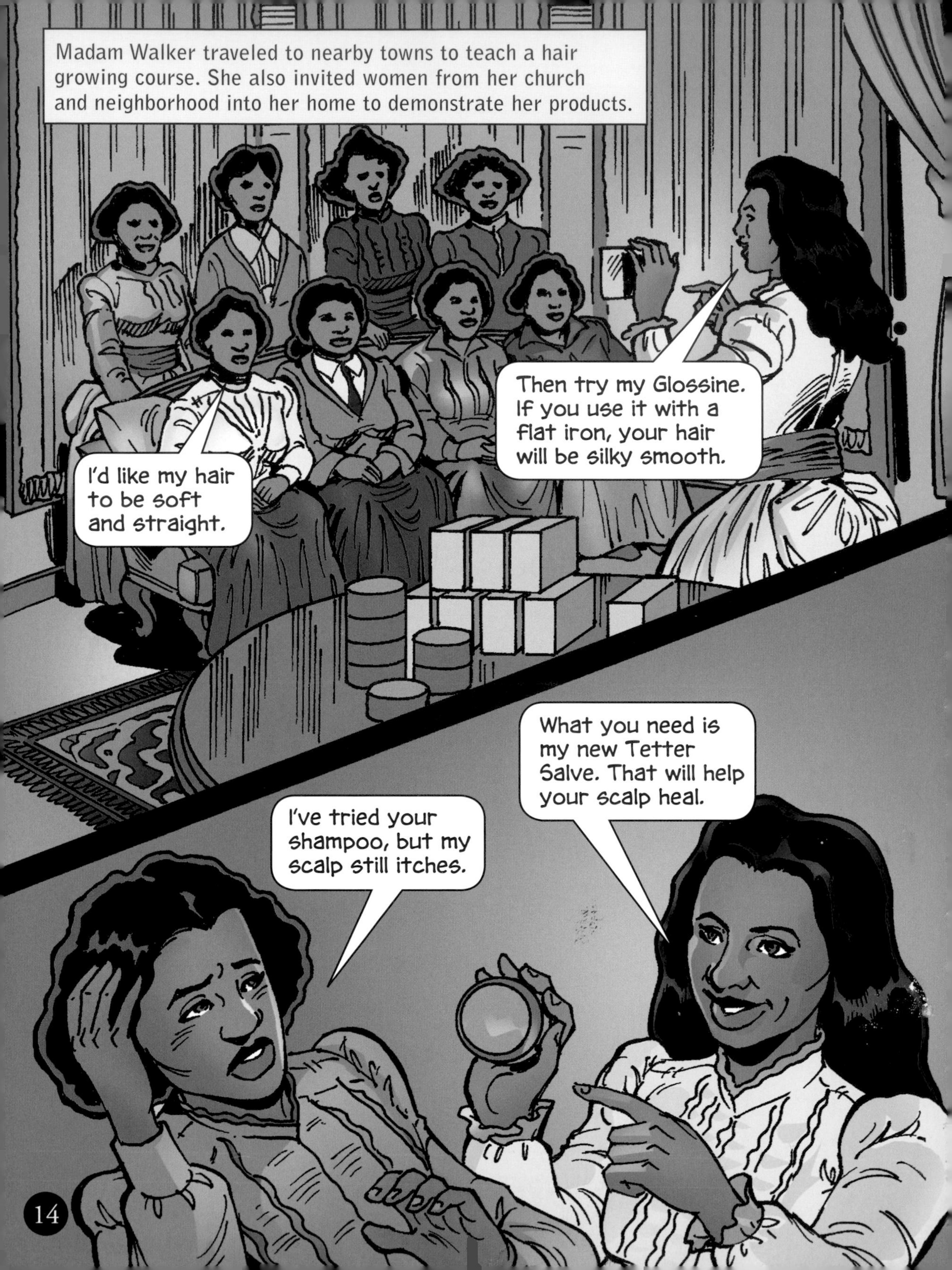
Madam Walker traveled to nearby towns to teach a hair growing course. She also invited women from her church and neighborhood into her home to demonstrate her products.
I'd like my hair to be soft and straight.
Then try my Glossine. If you use it with a flat iron, your hair will be silky smooth.
I've tried your shampoo, but my scalp still itches.
What you need is my new Tetter Salve. That will help your scalp heal.

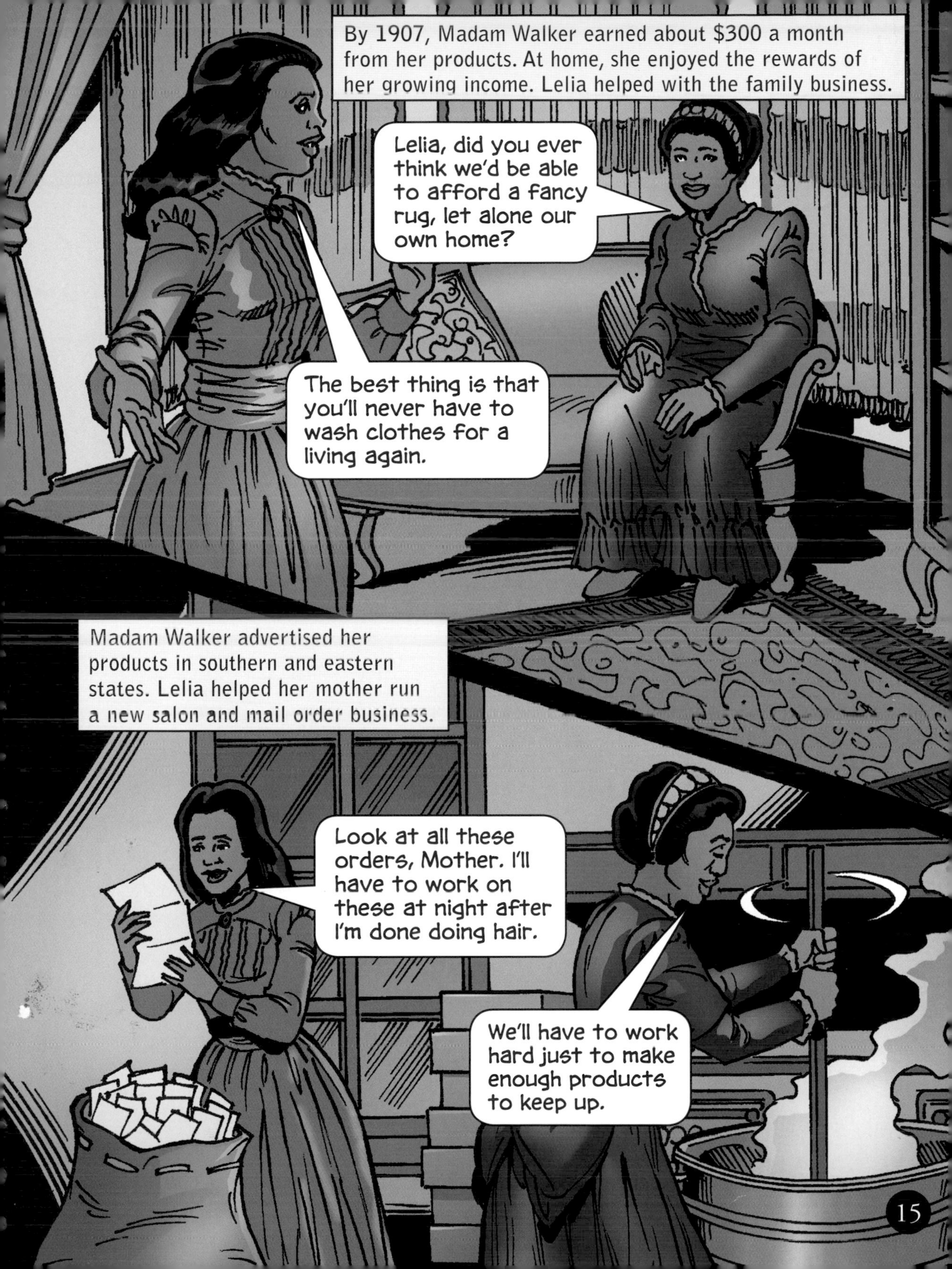
By 1907, Madam Walker earned about $300 a month from her products. At home, she enjoyed the rewards of her growing income. Lelia helped with the family business.
Lelia, did you ever think we'd be able to afford a fancy rug, let alone our own home?
The best thing is that you'll never have to wash clothes for a living again.
Madam Walker advertised her products in southern and eastern states. Lelia helped her mother run a new salon and mail order business.
Look at all these orders, Mother. I'll have to work on these at night after I'm done doing hair.
We'll have to work hard just to make enough products to keep up.

Chapter 3
Successful Woman

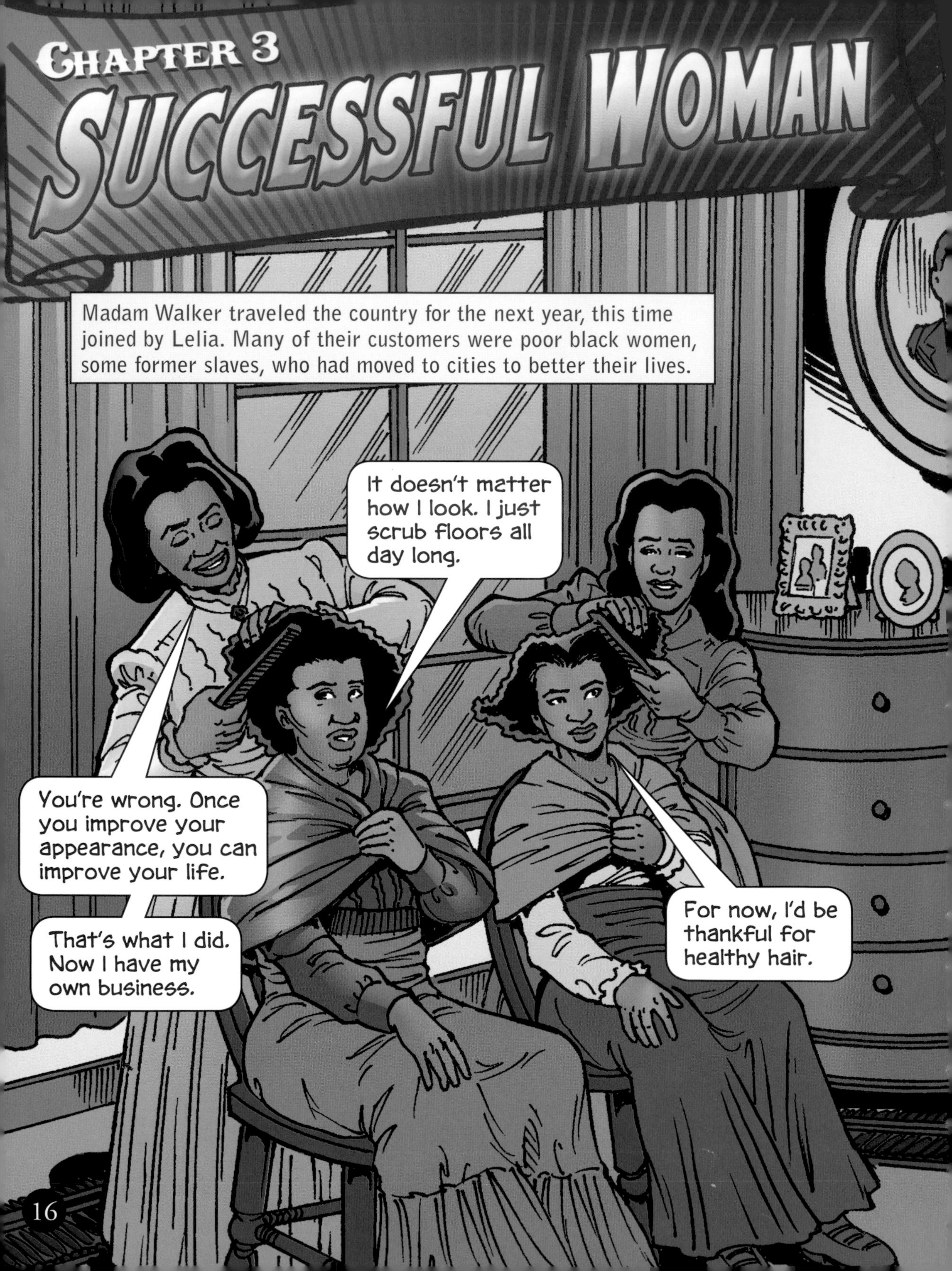

Madam Walker traveled the country for the next year, this time joined by Lelia. Many of their customers were poor black women, some former slaves, who had moved to cities to better their lives.
It doesn't matter how I look. I just scrub floors all day long.
You're wrong. Once you improve your appearance, you can improve your life.
That's what I did. Now I have my own business.
For now, I'd be thankful for healthy hair.

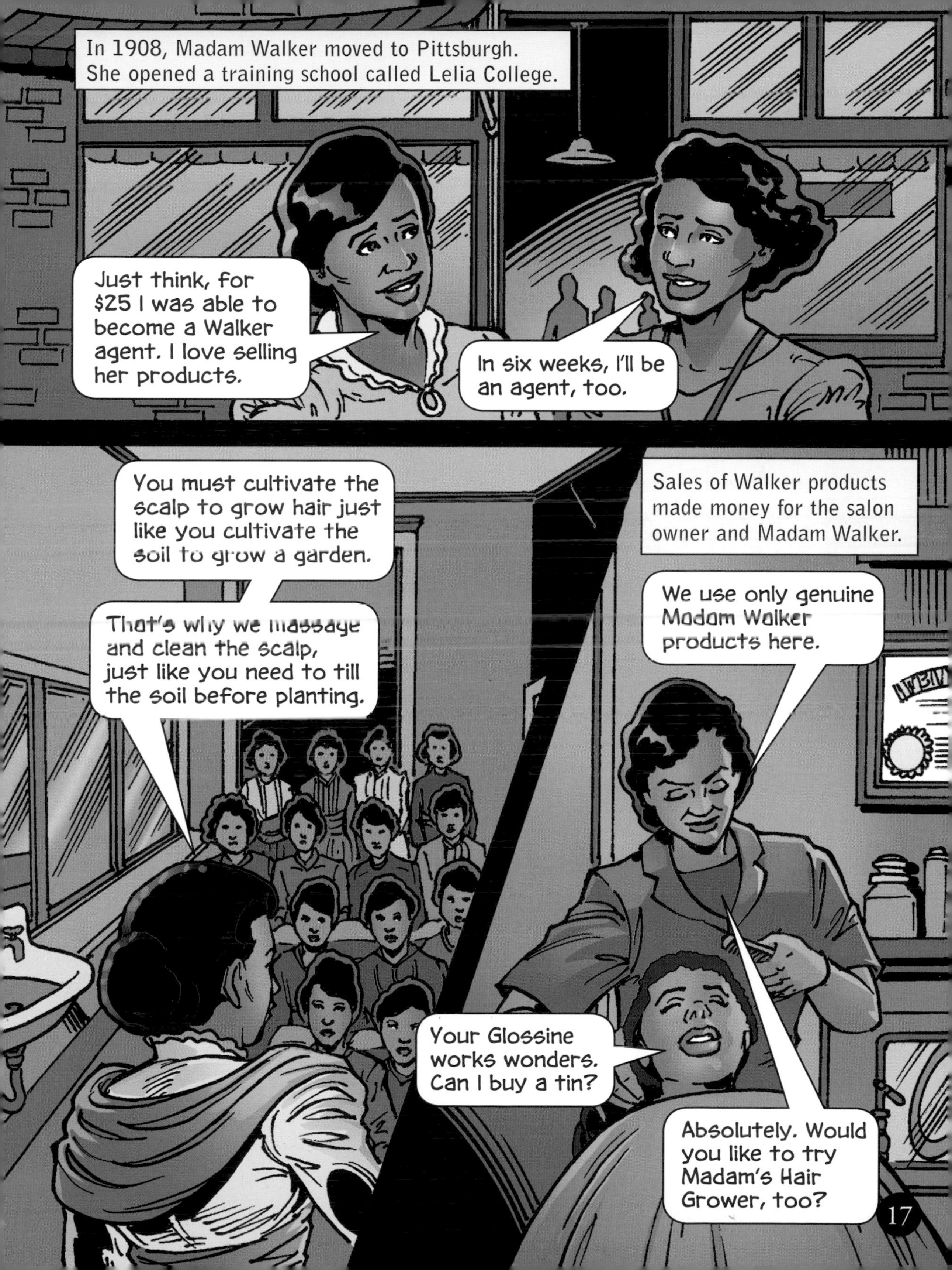
In 1908, Madam Walker moved to Pittsburgh. She opened a training school called Lelia College.
Just think, for $25 I was able to become a Walker agent. I love selling her products.
In six weeks, I'll be an agent, too.
You must cultivate the scalp to grow hair just like you cultivate the soil to grow a garden.
That's why we massage and clean the scalp, just like you need to till the soil before planting.
Sales of Walker products made money for the salon owner and Madam Walker.
We use only genuine Madam Walker products here.
Your Glossine works wonders. Can I buy a tin?
Absolutely. Would you like to try Madam's Hair Grower, too?

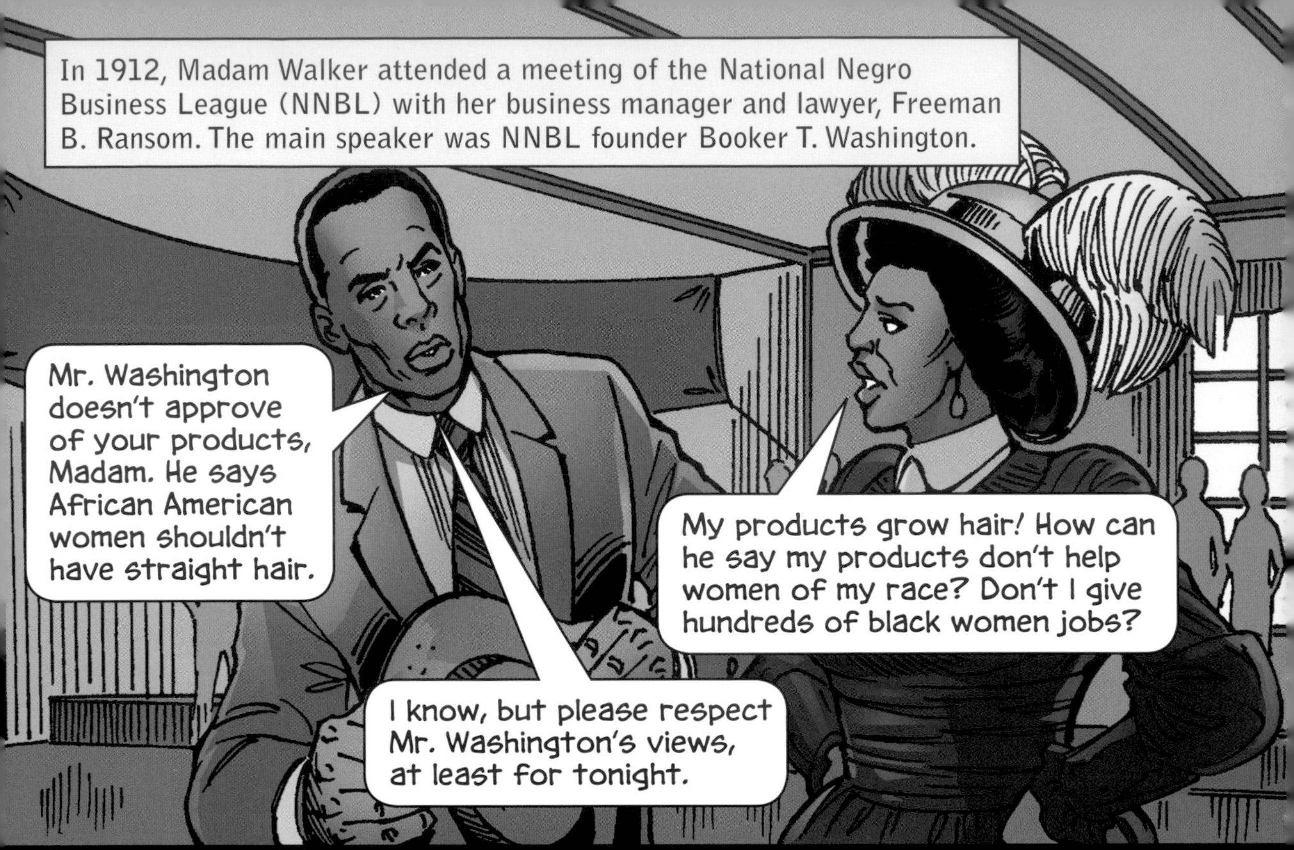
In 1912, Madam Walker attended a meeting of the National Negro Business League (NNBL) with her business manager and lawyer, Freeman B. Ransom. The main speaker was NNBL founder Booker T. Washington.
Mr. Washington doesn't approve of your products, Madam. He says African American women shouldn't have straight hair.
My products grow hair! How can he say my products don't help women of my race? Don't I give hundreds of black women jobs?
I know, but please respect Mr. Washington's views, at least for tonight.

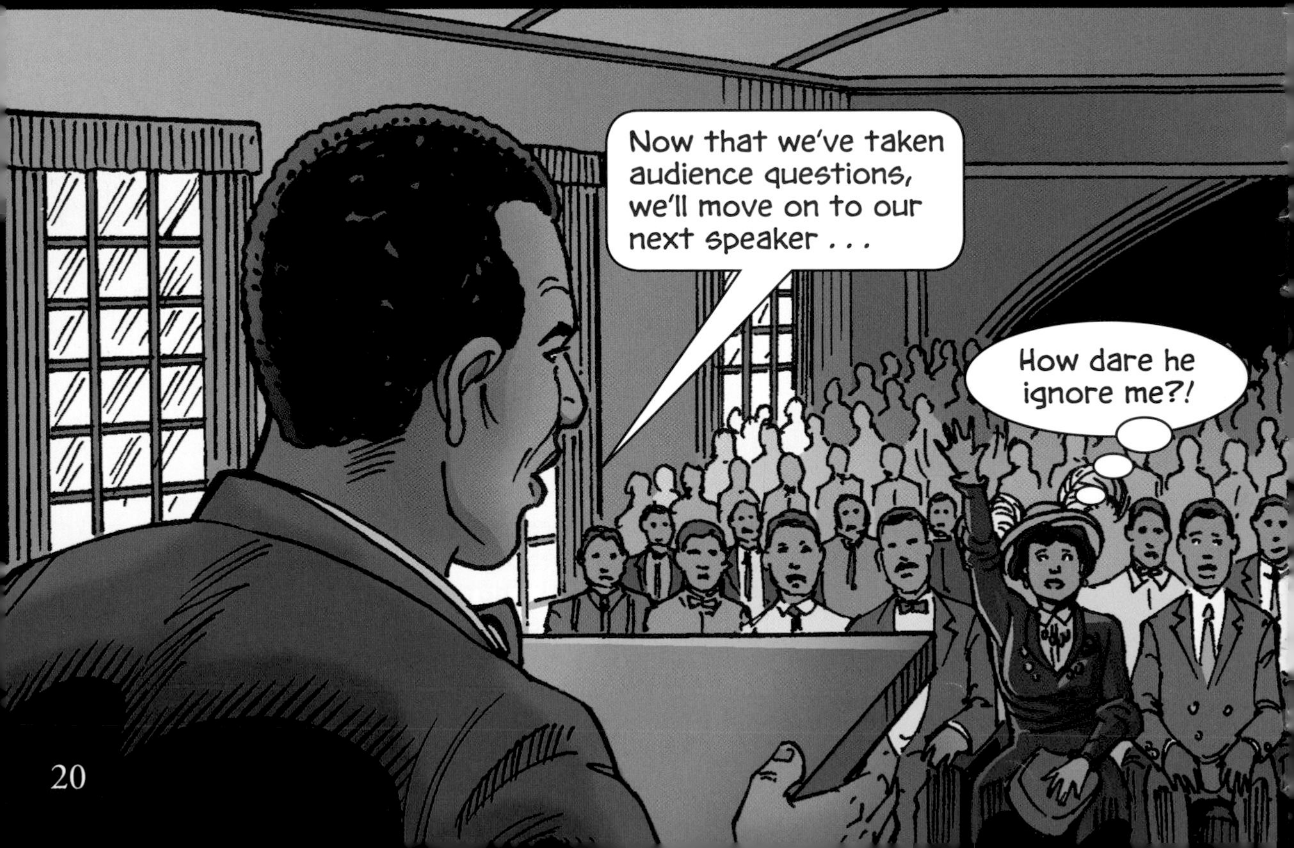
Now that we've taken audience questions, we'll move on to our next speaker . . .
How dare he ignore me?!

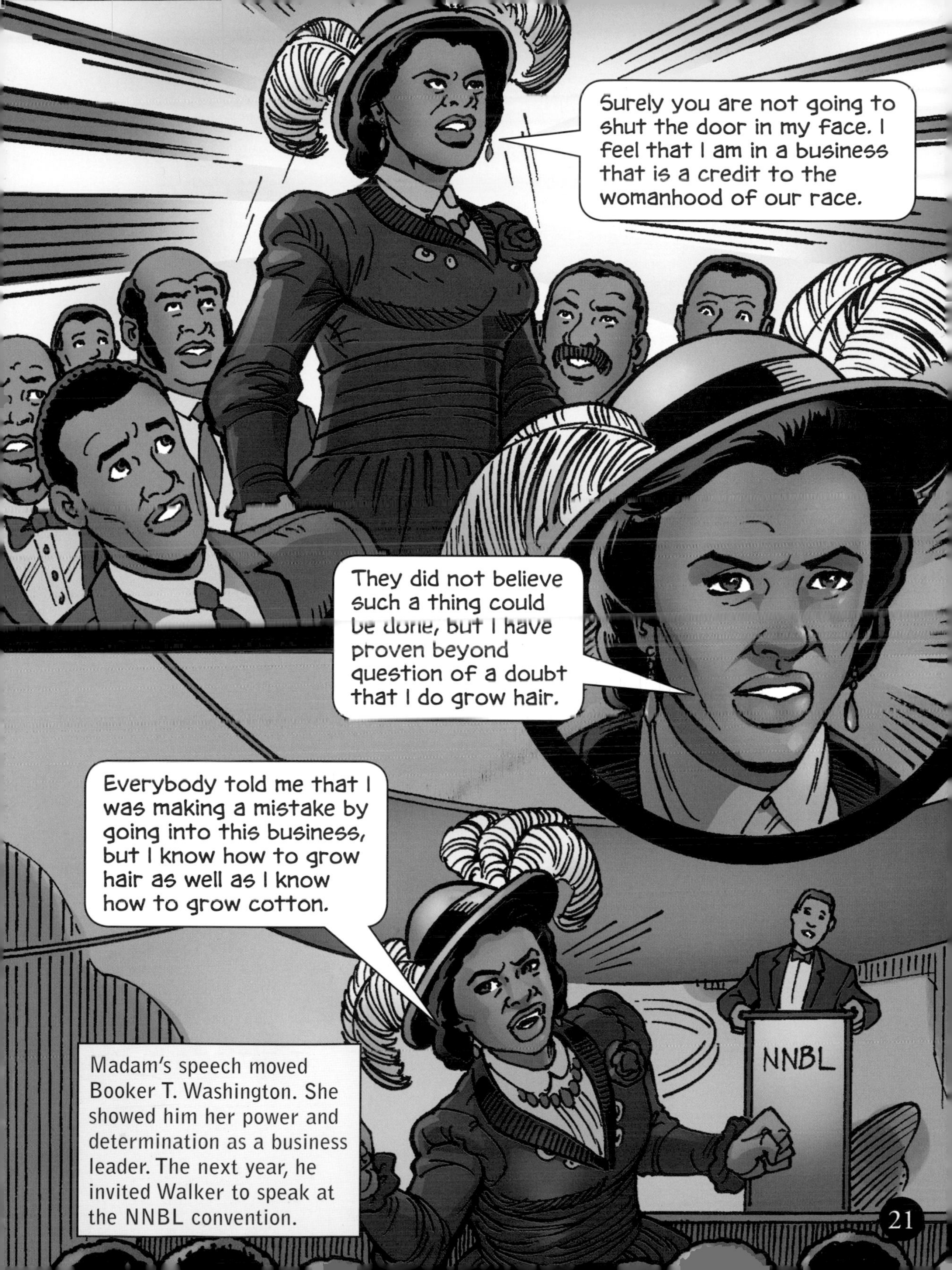
Surely you are not going to shut the door in my face. I feel that I am in a business that is a credit to the womanhood of our race.
They did not believe such a thing could be done, but I have proven beyond question of a doubt that I do grow hair.
Everybody told me that I was making a mistake by going into this business, but I know how to grow hair as well as I know how to grow cotton.
NNBL

Madam's speech moved Booker T. Washington. She showed him her power and determination as a business leader. The next year, he invited Walker to speak at the NNBL convention.

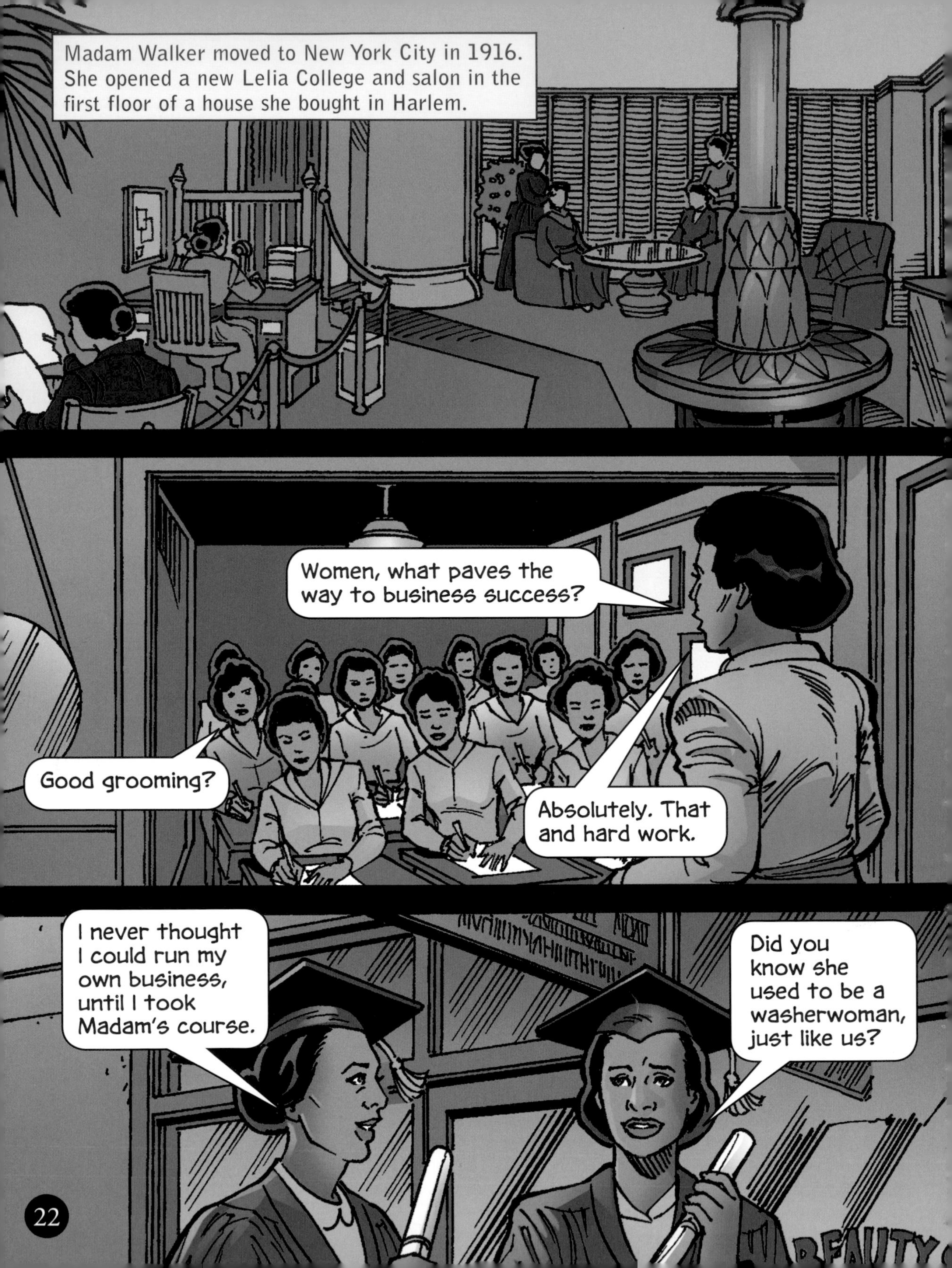
Madam Walker moved to New York City in 1916. She opened a new Lelia College and salon in the first floor of a house she bought in Harlem.
Women, what paves the way to business success?
Good grooming?
Absolutely. That and hard work.
I never thought I could run my own business, until I took Madam's course.
Did you know she used to be a washerwoman, just like us?

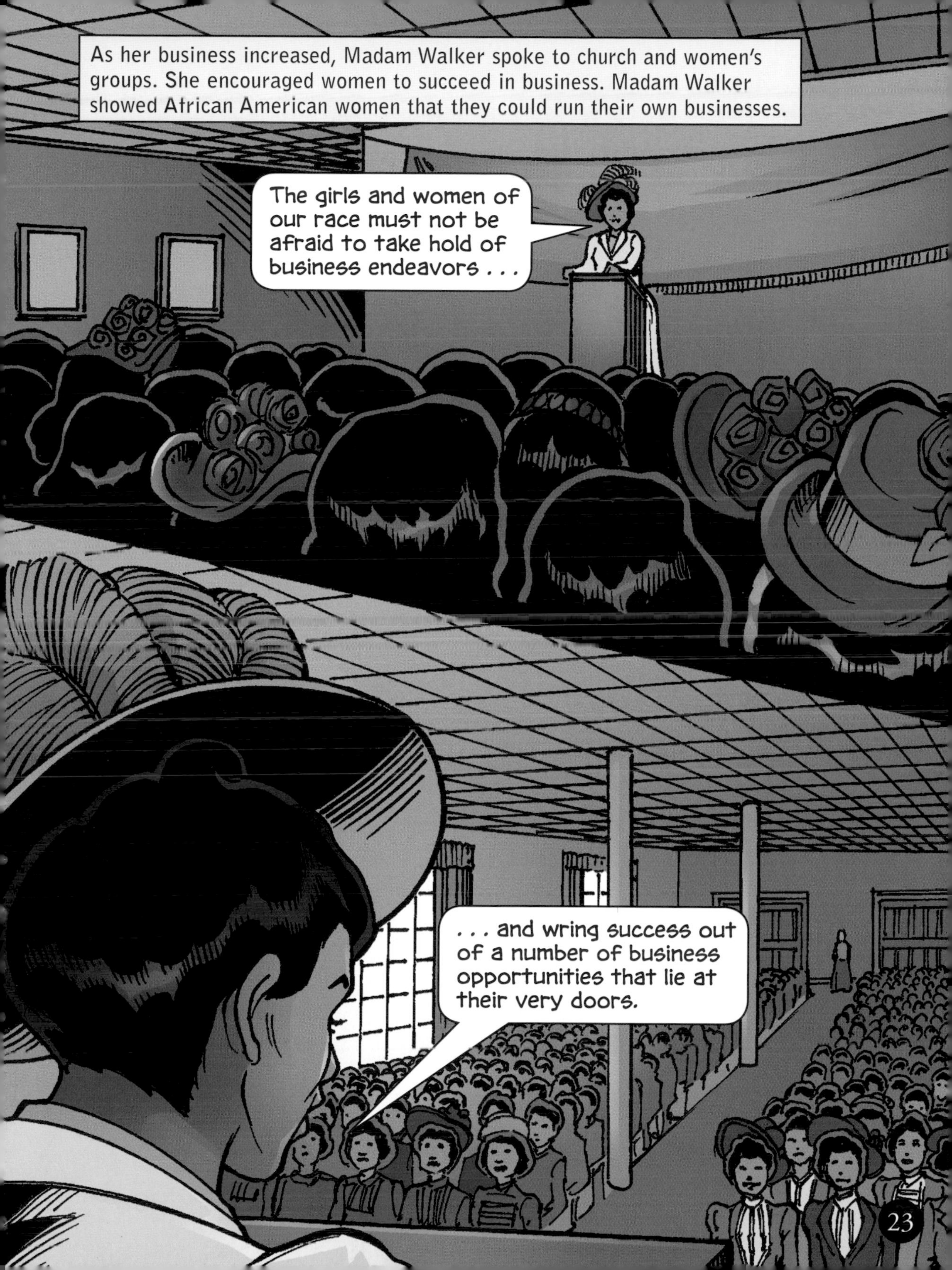
As her business increased, Madam Walker spoke to church and women's groups. She encouraged women to succeed in business. Madam Walker showed African American women that they could run their own businesses.
The girls and women of our race must not be afraid to take hold of business endeavors . . .
. . . and wring success out of a number of business opportunities that lie at their very doors.

Chapter 4
Lasting Legacy

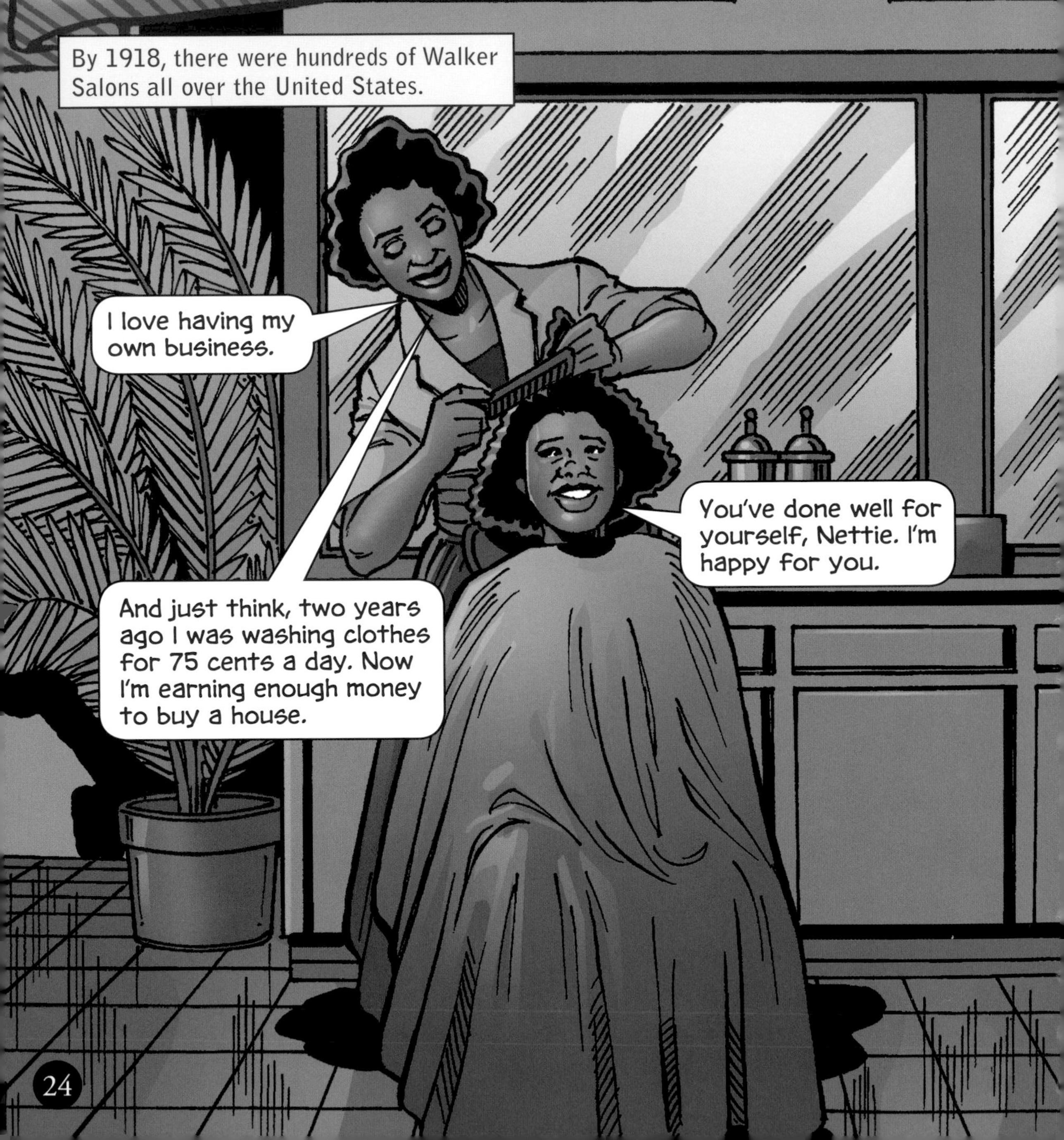
By 1918, there were hundreds of Walker Salons all over the United States.
I love having my own business.
And just think, two years ago I was washing clothes for 75 cents a day. Now I'm earning enough money to buy a house.
You've done well for yourself, Nettie. I'm happy for you.

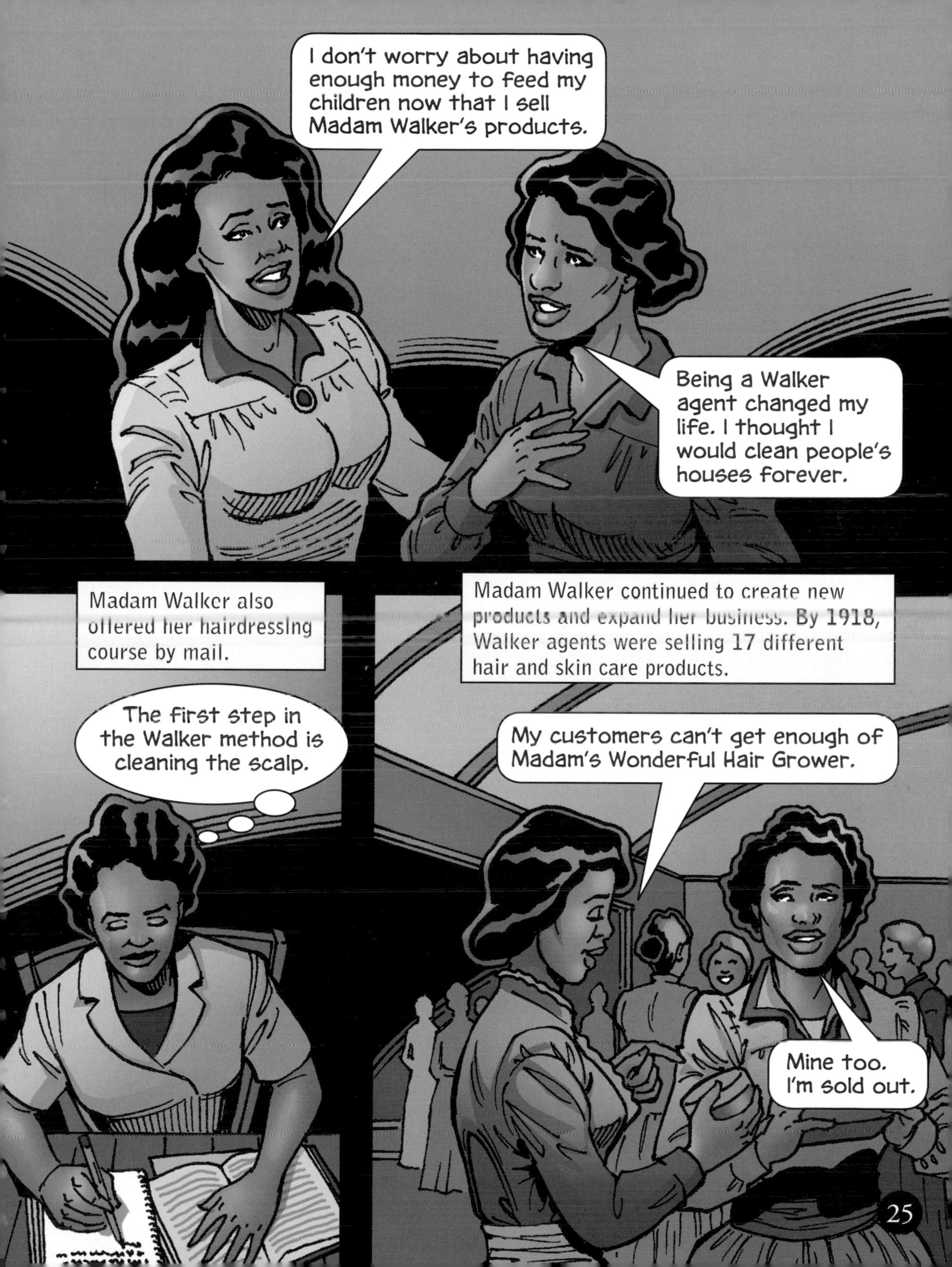
I don't worry about having enough money to feed my children now that I sell Madam Walker's products.
Being a Walker agent changed my life. I thought I would clean people's houses forever.
Madam Walker also offered her hairdressing course by mail.
The first step in the Walker method is cleaning the scalp.
Madam Walker continued to create new products and expand her business. By 1918, Walker agents were selling 17 different hair and skin care products.
My customers can't get enough of Madam's Wonderful Hair Grower.
Mine too. I'm sold out.

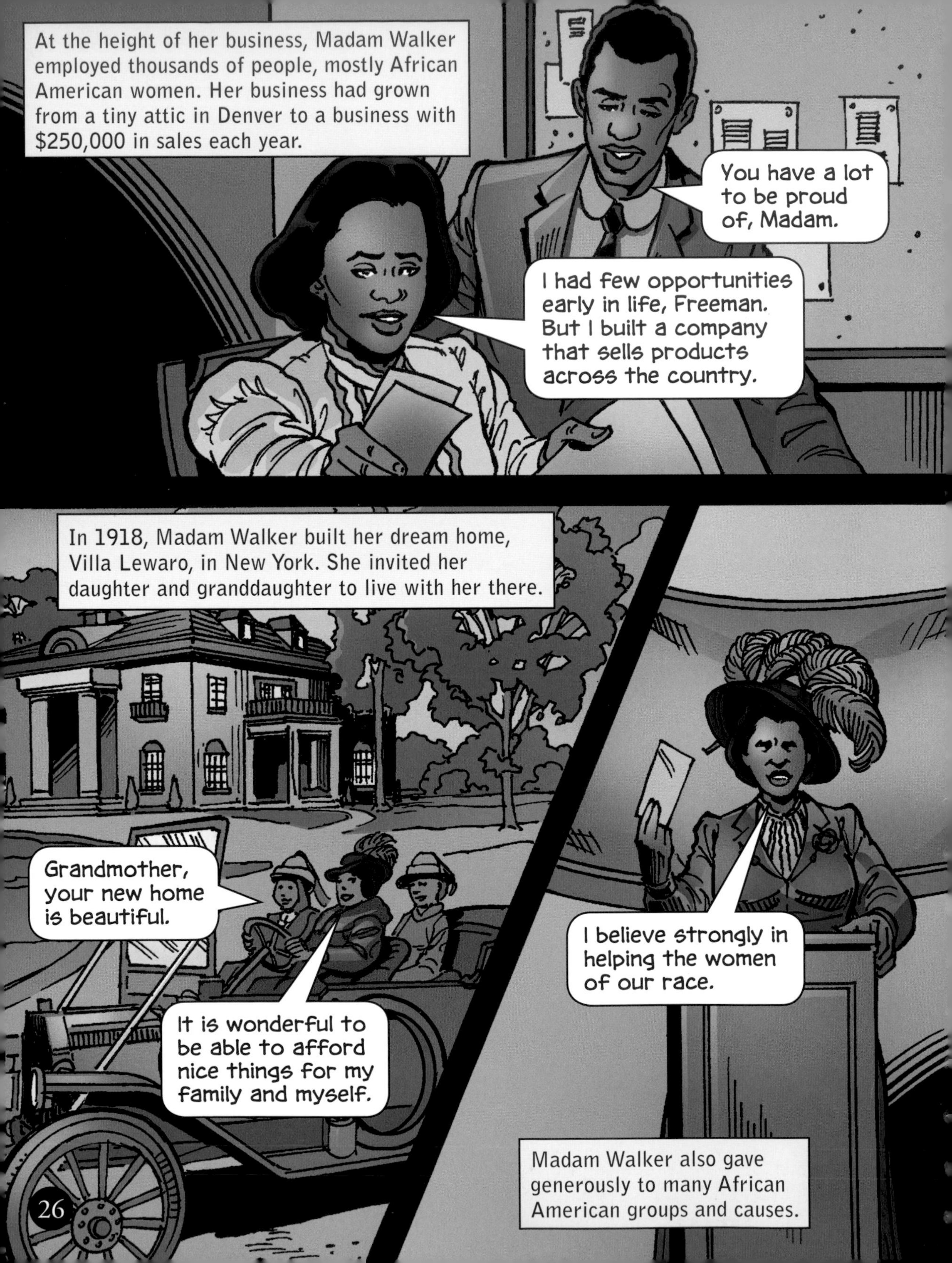
At the height of her business, Madam Walker employed thousands of people, mostly African American women. Her business had grown from a tiny attic in Denver to a business with $250,000 in sales each year.
You have a lot to be proud of, Madam.
I had few opportunities early in life, Freeman. But I built a company that sells products across the country.
In 1918, Madam Walker built her dream home, Villa Lewaro, in New York. She invited her daughter and granddaughter to live with her there.
Grandmother, your new home is beautiful.
It is wonderful to be able to afford nice things for my family and myself.
I believe strongly in helping the women of our race.
Madam Walker also gave generously to many African American groups and causes.

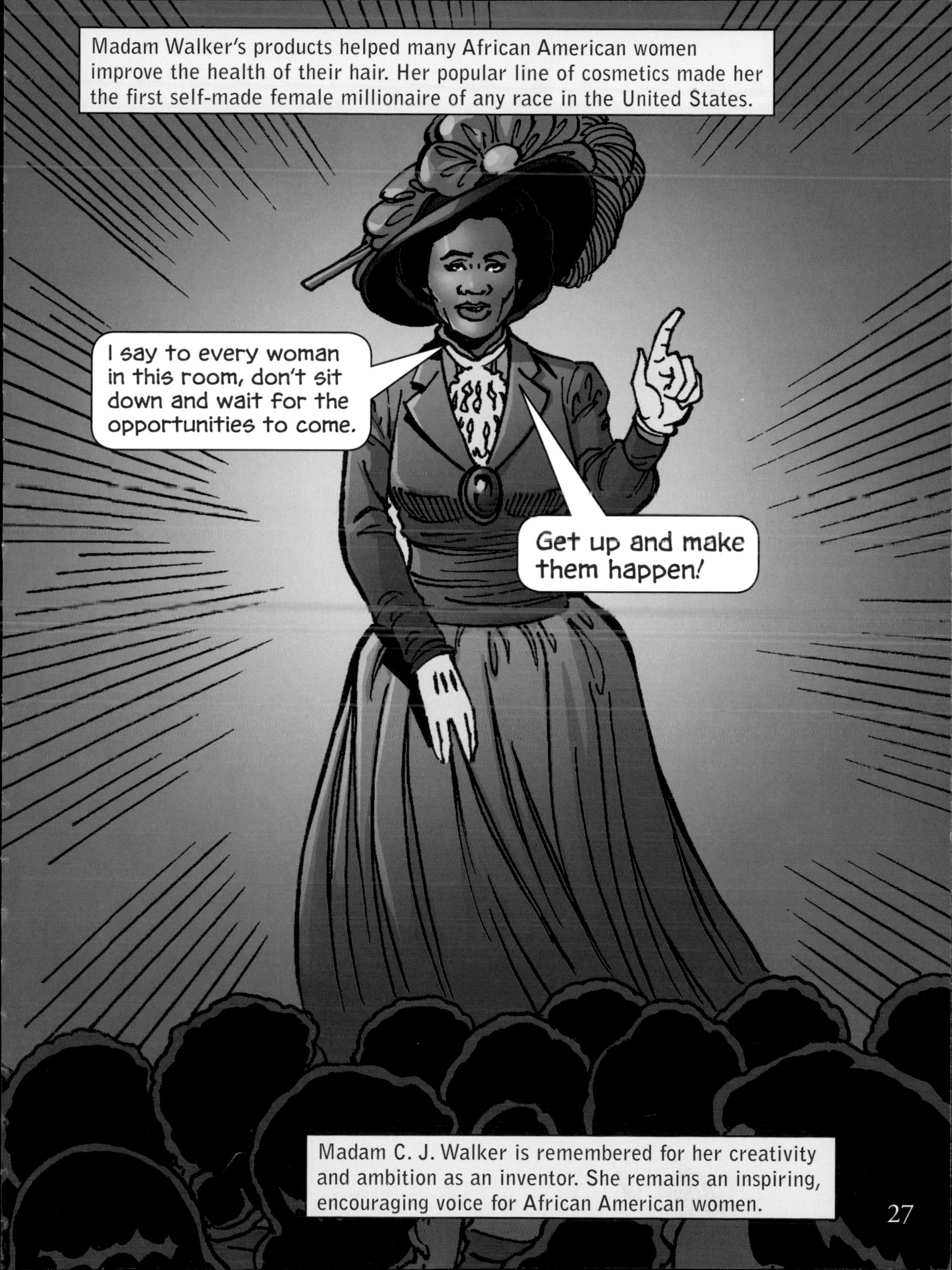
Madam Walker's products helped many African American women improve the health of their hair. Her popular line of cosmetics made her the first self-made female millionaire of any race in the United States.
I say to every woman in this room, don't sit down and wait for the opportunities to come.
Get up and make them happen!
Madam C. J. Walker is remembered for her creativity and ambition as an inventor. She remains an inspiring, encouraging voice for African American women.

MORE ABOUT MADAM C. J. WALKER

 Madam C. J. Walker was born Sarah Breedlove in 1867, in Louisiana. Her parents, Owen and Minerva, were sharecroppers and former slaves. Walker was the first person in her family to be born free.

Madam Walker was orphaned at age 6, married at 14, and had her only child, Lelia, at 17. Madam Walker was a widow by age 20.

After she invented Wonderful Hair Grower, Madam Walker put together the packaging for her product. She bought tins from the American Can Company. A man from her church, who owned a printing press, printed labels for the tins.

Some people falsely believe that Madam Walker invented the hair straightening comb. However, she did use a wide-toothed steel comb, heated on a stove, with Glossine. This method made hair look longer and straighter.

- Madam Walker created the Madam Walker Beauty Culturists Union. Each member paid yearly dues. The money helped employees in times of need.

- Madam Walker died on May 25, 1919. Her last words were, "I want to live to help my race."

- After her mother's death, Lelia ran the cosmetics company. Lelia died in 1931. The company remained in the Walker family until 1985 when the business was sold.

- Today, Madam Walker's Indianapolis factory is a National Historic Landmark. The building houses the Madam Walker Theater Center, a center for African American art and culture. Madam Walker's mansion, Villa Lewaro, is also a National Historic Landmark. The home is a private residence.

- In 1998, the United States Post Office released a postage stamp honoring Madam C. J. Walker.

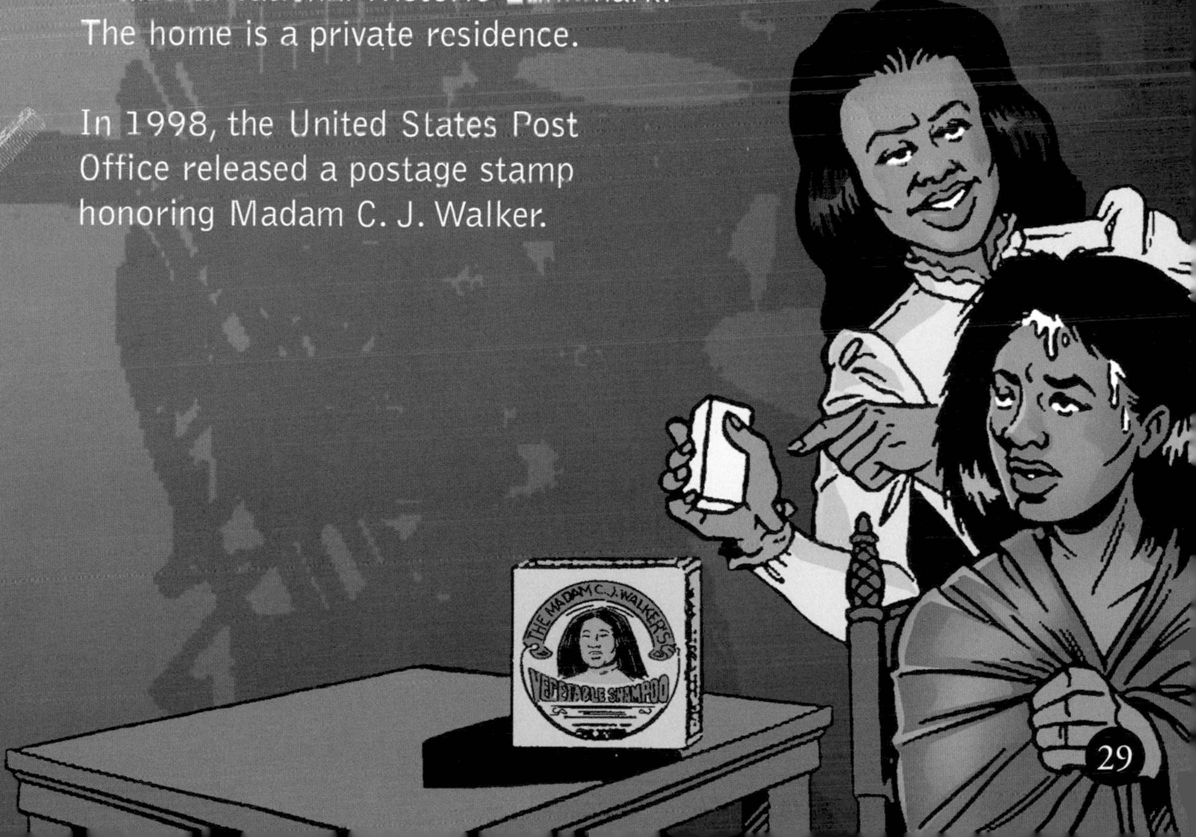
THE MADAM C. J. WALKER'S
VEGETABLE SHAMPOO

GLOSSARY

agent (AY-juhnt)—someone who arranges or sells things for other people

demonstrate (DEM-uhn-strate)—to show other people how to do something or use something

scalp treatment (SKALP TREET-muhnt)—the process of applying products to the head to help heal sores

sulfur (SUHL-fur)—a yellow chemical sometimes used to treat skin diseases

tetter (TET-tur)—a skin disease, often of the scalp, that causes sores and itching

tonic (TON-ik)—a liquid sometimes used to heal skin diseases

INTERNET SITES

FactHound offers a safe, fun way to find Internet sites related to this book. All of the sites on FactHound have been researched by our staff.

Here's how:
1. Visit *www.facthound.com*
2. Choose your grade level.
3. Type in this book ID **0736864857** for age-appropriate sites. You may also browse subjects by clicking on letters, or by clicking on pictures and words.
4. Click on the **Fetch It** button.

FactHound will fetch the best sites for you!

READ MORE

Hall, Margaret. *Madam C. J. Walker.* Lives and Times. Chicago: Heinemann, 2003.

Hobkirk, Lori. *Madam C. J. Walker.* Journey to Freedom. Chanhassen, Minn.: Child's World, 2001.

McKissack, Patricia, and Fredrick McKissak. *Madam C. J. Walker*: *Self-Made Millionaire.* Great African Americans. Berkeley Heights, N.J.: Enslow, 2001.

Nichols, Catherine. *Madam C. J. Walker.* Scholastic News Nonfiction Readers. New York: Children's Press, 2005.

Sullivan, Otha Richard. *African American Women Scientists and Inventors.* Black Stars. New York: Wiley, 2002.

BIBLIOGRAPHY

Bundles, A'Lelia. *On Her Own Ground: The Life and Times of Madam C. J. Walker.* New York: Scribner, 2001.

Madam C. J. Walker Papers. Indiana Historical Society, Indianapolis, Ind. (http://www.indianahistory.org/library/manuscripts/collection_guides/m0399.html)

INDEX